INVISIBLE BAGS

INVISIBLE BAGS

For Women Who Carry Too Much

Dr. Tarcia Gilliam Parrish

The Invisible Work Series

A three-book journey exploring interruption, the unseen weight women carry, and the quiet authority that emerges through growth.

Woman, Interrupted

Reclaiming Purpose, Power, and Peace After Life's Unexpected Pauses

Invisible Bags

For Women Who Carry Too Much

Invisible Work

The Quiet Authority of Becoming

Invisible Bags

For Women Who Carry Too Much

Published by The Power of Engagement

Memphis, TN 38111

Website: www.thepowerofengagement.com

Book cover: Kylan, The Kreator kylanthekreator@gmail.com

Print ISBN: 978-1-964663-20-3

Library of Congress Control Number: 2025928217

First Edition: 2026

Dedication

This book is dedicated to the women who have carried more than anyone ever acknowledged. The women who quietly absorbed expectations, responsibilities, emotional labor, and invisible obligations because someone had to hold everything together.

Many of these burdens were never discussed, yet they shaped how you moved through rooms, relationships, and responsibilities. If you have ever found yourself exhausted from holding what others overlooked, this work invites you to pause and examine what you are carrying and why.

These pages are an invitation to name the weight, question its origin, and release what yours was never to sustain. The work begins when you recognize that strength is not proven by how much you can carry, but by the wisdom to put things down.

Contents

Letter to the Reader

Dear Reader,

This book was written gently. It was not written to rush you toward change or to suggest that everything you have carried must suddenly be put down. Many of the things' women carry were taken on for meaningful reasons. They were connected to love, responsibility, survival, leadership, and the quiet determination to keep life moving forward when stopping was not an option.

Across families, workplaces, communities, and relationships, women have learned to carry what was needed to keep things stable. They carried inherited expectations about strength. They stepped into roles where they became the ones others relied on. They held unspoken hurt so relationships could continue. They absorbed responsibility so systems would not fall apart.

Often, these responsibilities were never formally assigned. They appeared gradually through trust, necessity, and expectation. Over time, what began as a moment of support became a pattern of endurance.

This book refers to those patterns as "invisible bags."

Some are inherited through generations that equate strength with survival. Some grow from leadership roles where responsibility expands faster than support. Others form through silence, when hurt was never given language and therefore never given the chance to heal.

These invisible bags do not always feel heavy at first. Many women learn to carry them so skillfully that the weight becomes almost invisible. Being dependable becomes identity. Endurance becomes normal. Responsibility becomes proof of capability. Yet even the strongest shoulders feel the weight of what has been carried for too long.

This book does not assume that every woman's experience is the same. The stories, responsibilities, and expectations that shape our lives differ widely. But many women share a common pattern: learning to carry more than they were ever meant to hold alone.

These pages offer space to recognize those patterns.

You will encounter reflections about inherited strength and the expectation to endure. You will explore the quiet labor of being the one who holds things together. You will consider the weight of unspoken hurt that settles when pain is never acknowledged. Later, the book turns toward the deeper work of confronting what has been carried, understanding its cost, and deciding what still belongs to you.

Eventually, the focus shifts toward something new: releasing unnecessary weight and redefining what strength can look like moving forward.

None of this requires urgency. This book is not a demand for transformation. It is an invitation to pause long enough to notice what you have been holding.

Some pages may feel like mirrors reflecting experiences you have quietly carried.

Some may feel a sense of permission to question expectations that once felt permanent. Some may feel like a release. Take what you need. Pause when you need to. Put the rest down.

With care,

Dr. Tarcia Gilliam-Parrish

Introduction

Naming What We Carry

Naming What We Carry

Before we go any further, pause and notice what you are carrying.

Every woman carries something invisible. Not because she wants to, but because she learned that if she did not, things would fall apart. Families would unravel. Work would suffer. People would be disappointed. So, women carry. And they keep carrying even when they are tired, resentful, overwhelmed, and depleted.

Many women hate the weight they carry yet feel unable to stop carrying it. Carrying becomes proof of love, responsibility, strength, and worth. Over time, doing everything begins to feel like a superpower. Being the one who can handle it all becomes part of identity. What is rarely acknowledged is that this so-called superpower slowly weakens women until there is very little left for themselves.

Written for women who have been praised for their endurance but never protected from overload, these pages name a truth many recognize only after the cost has already been paid. Invisible bags are often placed on women long before there is choice or awareness. Some are handed over through expectation. Others are picked up slowly in the name of love, survival, leadership, or obligation.

Most women do not realize what they are carrying until the weight becomes undeniable. Sometimes the reckoning arrives as illness. Sometimes it is burnout. Sometimes it is an emotional collapse. Sometimes it comes quietly, one morning, as the realization that everything has been given to everyone else and nothing is left for oneself. Sometimes it comes dressed well, but hiding bruises from the night before.

Women have been taught to set themselves on fire to keep others warm. That pattern has been normalized, praised, and rewarded, especially for those who lead, nurture, and serve. Naming that truth is not weakness. Stopping is not selfish. Continuing without question is what causes harm.

These pages do not suggest, “You learned this, so simply unlearn it.” They acknowledge, “This was done to you, reinforced around you, and normalized. Now it must be named so it can be interrupted.” The message speaks to women who have learned to absorb emotional labor, manage relationships, lead under pressure, and hold everything together quietly.

Although written with women in mind, anyone who has loved, worked alongside, or depended on women may recognize these patterns and learn from them.

The focus is not merely on carrying burdens. It examines gendered expectations, emotional labor placed disproportionately on women, social conditioning that rewards endurance, leadership roles where invisible work is absorbed without acknowledgment, and the ways guilt, self-erasure, and over functioning are taught as virtues.

Throughout these pages, "burden" refers to emotional or mental weight that is not intentionally chosen. Endurance refers to surviving through constant pushing without relief. Capacity refers to the emotional, physical, and mental space required to function without harm. Leadership refers to responsibility carried without self-erasure.

Each chapter invites readers to notice what they are carrying, name how it was placed on them or slowly picked up and decide what can no longer be taken without cost. Perfection and urgency are not required. There is permission to receive what is helpful and gently release the invisible bags that no longer serve.

Release may happen one bag at a time or through a clean break. Both are valid. What matters is no longer carrying what is costing you yourself.

You are not broken. You were set on fire to keep others warm.

You are burdened.

And burdens, whether placed on you or picked up in the course of survival, can be put down.

Not because they want to, but because somewhere along the way, they learned that if they did not, things would fall apart. Families would unravel. Work would suffer. Relationships would strain. Needs would go unmet. So, women carry. And they keep carrying even when they are tired, resentful, overwhelmed, and depleted.

Many women dislike the weight they carry yet feel unable to stop carrying it. Carrying becomes proof of love, responsibility, strength, and worth. Over time, doing everything begins to feel like a superpower. Being the one who can handle it all becomes part of identity. What is rarely acknowledged is that this so-called superpower slowly weakens women until there is very little left for themselves.

These pages confront the invisible bags. The emotional weight. The expectations. The unspoken roles. The responsibilities were assumed without consent. The strength is inherited without rest.

Here, burden refers to emotional or mental weight that is not intentionally chosen but is carried out of necessity or expectation. Endurance refers to the learned ability to push through without support. Capacity refers to the emotional, physical, and mental space required to function without harm.

The message is not that women should stop caring or stop leading. It questions the belief that everything depends on them alone.

Chapter One explores inherited strength and how endurance often became a requirement rather than a choice. Many women learned early that being dependable meant carrying what others could not. What began as survival gradually became expectation, shaping how strength and responsibility were understood.

Chapter Two examines the role of being "the one" and how leadership labor and overcommitment can quietly transform capable women into overloaded ones. When competence is consistently rewarded with more responsibility, leadership can shift from influence on constant stabilization.

Chapter Three addresses the quiet weight of unspoken hurt and what happens when pain is never given language. When experiences are minimized or left unresolved, women often continue to function outwardly while carrying an emotional weight that remains unseen.

Chapter Four focuses on the point at which carrying becomes harmful, and the body begins to respond to what has been held too long. Fatigue, tension, and emotional exhaustion often reveal what endurance has concealed.

Chapter Five reframes letting go as a form of leadership rather than failure. Releasing unnecessary responsibility allows systems to grow and invites others to share responsibility.

Chapter Six rebuilds confidence and worth apart from productivity. Women begin to rediscover identity beyond what they accomplish, produce, or hold together for others.

Chapter Seven offers a vision for living lighter and leading freer without guilt. It explores what becomes possible when strength includes rest, boundaries, and the freedom to choose what truly belongs.

Chapter Eight reminds us that no person was ever meant to carry everything alone. Responsibility functions best when it is shared, and leadership becomes sustainable when weight is distributed rather than concentrated in one place.

Chapter Nine focuses on carrying life forward with intention. Awareness becomes practice as women continue choosing what aligns with their values while releasing what no longer belongs to them.

Although written with women in mind, anyone who has loved, worked alongside, or relied on women may recognize these patterns and learn from them.

You are not broken.
You are burdened.
And burdens can be put down.

PART I: RECOGNIZING THE INVISIBLE BAGS

Before a bag can be released, it must first be recognized. Many of the burden's women carry are invisible, not because they are small, but because they have been normalized. Expectations, responsibilities, emotional labor, and unspoken obligations accumulate over time. They are carried quietly, often without acknowledgment, and eventually shape how a woman sees herself and moves through the world.

Invisible bags are formed through roles, relationships, and experiences that require strength without always offering support. They can include the pressure to remain composed, the responsibility to hold families together, the expectation to perform without complaint, and the habit of prioritizing others' needs over one's own. Because these burdens are rarely named, they often go unquestioned.

Part I invites readers to pause and examine what they have been carrying. Recognition is not about blame. It is about awareness. When a woman becomes conscious of the invisible bags she carries, she gains the clarity necessary to begin to understand their weight and origin.

Awareness is the first step toward freedom. What is named can be examined. What is examined can eventually be transformed.

CHAPTER 1

Inherited Strength and the Expectation to Endure

Inherited Strength and the Expectation to Endure

Many women inherit strength before they inherit language. Long before they understand choice, they learn responsibility. Endurance becomes an expectation rather than a decision. Silence becomes protection. Rest becomes optional. In many families and communities, strength was never presented as a preference. It was presented as a requirement.

From an early age, women are taught how to hold things together. They learn how to help, anticipate needs, and manage difficult moments without drawing attention to themselves. They learn how to absorb tension in a room, comfort others, and remain steady when circumstances feel uncertain. These lessons are rarely written down or formally explained. They are learned through observation, repetition, and quiet expectation.

Many women grew up watching the women before them carry extraordinary responsibility without visible relief. Mothers, grandmothers, and caretakers moved through hardship with determination, rarely pausing long enough to name the weight they were carrying. Younger generations absorbed these patterns as examples of what strength looked like. Survival became the model. Endurance became the measure of character.

These lessons were not given out of cruelty. They were forms of protection shaped by difficult circumstances. Women who came before often lived in environments where vulnerability was unsafe, and support was limited. Silence protected dignity. Self-reliance protected stability. Strength ensured that families continued moving forward even when conditions were uncertain.

What once preserved life, however, can later restrict it. Survival strategies developed in one generation can quietly become emotional obligations in the next. When endurance becomes identity, it can be difficult to imagine another way of living. Strength becomes something a woman feels she must constantly prove, even when the circumstances that required such constant endurance have changed.

Resilience can be honored without carrying exhaustion forever. The endurance passed down through generations deserves respect, yet it also deserves reflection. Understanding how inherited patterns continue to shape the present allows women to keep the wisdom of resilience while loosening the grip of constant strain.

What many women quietly carry can be understood as the invisible bag of inherited strength. Research on women, resilience, and generational survival often shows that women are praised for endurance while rarely being offered relief. The praise is real, but the support is often limited. Over time, endurance becomes expected, and relief begins to feel undeserved.

While every woman's experience is different, many share a similar internal belief: stopping feels dangerous. Pausing can feel like neglect. Rest can feel like failure. When strength has been tied to survival for generations, slowing down can feel unfamiliar and uncomfortable.

The invisible bag of inherited strength often appears in daily life as constant availability. Women who carry it are frequently the first to respond when something goes wrong and the last to rest when a problem is resolved. They step into situations that require stability, often without being formally asked. They take responsibility for emotional balance in families, workplaces, and communities.

Much of this work happens quietly. Emotional labor, crisis management, conflict mediation, and relational maintenance rarely appear in job descriptions. Yet these responsibilities shape how family's function and how organizations operate. Women carrying this weight often absorb tension so others can continue moving forward without disruption.

Another way this burden appears is through the management of other people's emotional experiences. Women may find themselves holding stress, disappointment, or unresolved feelings that do not belong to them. They mediate conflicts they did not create. They soften conversations that might otherwise become confrontational. They carry guilt for situations outside their control simply to keep relationships stable.

This burden can also include unresolved relationships and situations that were never properly closed. Women may continue carrying emotional responsibility long after circumstances have changed. They replay conversations, question past decisions, or remain connected to roles that no longer fit their lives. The weight continues not because the responsibility still exists, but because the habit of carrying it remains.

In everyday life, inherited strength often shows up as difficulty saying no. Women may find themselves overcommitted, managing multiple responsibilities at once while feeling internal pressure to keep everything around them running. Rest may feel unearned. Stillness may feel uncomfortable. The absence of responsibility can feel unfamiliar, even when exhaustion is present.

In leadership and professional environments, this pattern often appears as over functioning. Women anticipate problems before they arise. They fill gaps when systems fail. They absorb tension so teams remain stable. They maintain emotional balance within groups so others can focus on their roles. What others see as competence or reliability may internally feel like constant pressure to hold everything together.

Over time, this invisible burden can begin to shape identity. Being dependable becomes a defining trait. Being the one who handles things is how others recognize and rely on her. Yet what often goes unnamed is how much of her own emotional space becomes occupied by responsibilities that were never fully hers to carry.

Why We Carry It

Women carry this bag because endurance was modeled as love and responsibility. Strength became a form of safety. In many families, the women who held everything together were the ones who were admired, depended on, and remembered as strong. Responsibility became a way of expressing care.

For many women, letting go can feel like a betrayal of the women who survived before them. The strength that allowed previous generations to endure difficult circumstances created a powerful legacy. Carrying the same weight can feel like honoring that legacy, even when the burden becomes overwhelming.

The message passed quietly across generations is simple. Strong women keep going. They do not stop when they are tired. They do not place their needs ahead of others. They hold families together, manage crises, and absorb hardship so others can remain stable.

Over time, these expectations become internalized. A woman may continue carrying more than she should, not because anyone asked her to, but because the role has become familiar. Responsibility feels natural. Rest feels uncertain.

What This Bag Costs

Carrying inherited strength without relief creates an emotional deficit. Women may appear capable, steady, and dependable on the outside while feeling quietly depleted on the inside. When the body and mind remain in a constant state of responsibility, something important begins to narrow.

Joy becomes smaller. Creativity fades. Personal desires are postponed until there is time that never quite arrives. The voice that once spoke clearly about needs and boundaries grows quieter as responsibility grows louder.

The body often absorbs what the voice never releases. Fatigue becomes normal. Stress settles into muscles, sleep patterns, and concentration. When exhaustion becomes familiar, many women stop recognizing how deeply it has affected them.

The cost extends beyond the woman herself. Relationships can become strained when exhaustion turns into quiet resentment. Leadership can become rigid when fatigue replaces reflection. Collaboration becomes more difficult when emotional capacity has already been spent managing constant responsibility.

Moving Forward

Inherited strength was never meant to become a permanent burden. It was meant to carry women through difficult seasons until new possibilities became available. The endurance passed down through generations helped families survive. It helped communities remain stable. It helped women move forward even when circumstances were uncertain.

Survival, however, was never meant to be the only way of living.

The lessons of endurance taught women how to withstand pressure, remain steady during hardship, and continue when stopping was not an option. Those lessons-built resilience, determination, and courage. Yet strength was never meant to require constant exhaustion.

There comes a point when endurance must evolve. The same strength that once required silence can begin to support honesty. The resilience that once demanded constant motion can begin to allow rest. Strength does not disappear when the weight is set down. It becomes more intentional.

Wanting more ease does not dishonor the women who survived before you. Recognizing the weight, you carry does not erase the resilience you inherited. Pausing to breathe, reflect, and reconsider what belongs to you is not weakness. It is wisdom.

The strength you inherited helped you stand when life demanded it. The strength you are developing now helps you choose how you want to live moving forward.

Endurance does not vanish when rest enters the picture. It transforms. What once looked like constant effort becomes discernment. You begin to recognize what is truly yours to carry and what was never meant to belong to you.

With that awareness comes space. Space for joy that is no longer postponed. Space for creativity that is no longer buried beneath responsibility. Space for relationships built on mutual care rather than quiet sacrifice.

The invisible bags many women carry do not appear overnight, and they rarely disappear all at once. Awareness opens the door to choice. Reflection creates the opportunity to decide which burdens still belong and which ones can finally be released.

The question is no longer whether you are strong enough to keep carrying everything.

The question becomes whether everything you are carrying was ever meant to be yours.

Reflection: Inherited Strength and the Expectation to Endure

Pause

Before responding to the prompts, take a moment to notice what thoughts or emotions surfaced while reading.

Guided Prompts

- What did the women before me survive that I am still carrying?
- Where do I confuse loyalty with self-sacrifice?
- How does rest challenge the way I was taught to be strong?
- What am I afraid might happen if I stop enduring?
- How can I honor my lineage without repeating their exhaustion?

Journaling

___

___

___

___

___

___

___

___

___

Carrying less makes room for growth. Strength does not have to mean suffering.

CHAPTER 2

Being "The One", Leadership Labor, and Overcommitment

Being "The One," Leadership Labor, and Overcommitment

Somewhere along the way, you became the one. The one who notices what is missing before anyone else does. The one who fills the gap without being asked. The one people rely on because you always find a way.

Being the one is rarely assigned. It develops through patterns of reliability. A person solves a problem, offers support, or brings clarity during a moment of uncertainty. When that response happens repeatedly, people begin to recognize it. Eventually, they expect it.

Over time, the role becomes attached to the person rather than the situation. The one who becomes the first-person people call when something goes wrong. The one who knows the answer, who organizes the solution, or who steps forward when others hesitate.

Being the one often brings trust and respect. People value the person who can steady the environment and move things forward. Yet the role can also expand quietly and continuously. What began as an initiative becomes a responsibility. What began as a responsibility becomes an expectation.

Without intention, being the one can slowly become an identity. Others begin to rely on your presence for stability. They wait for your response before acting. They assume you will carry what others leave behind.

The strength required to hold that role is real. But so is the weight.

Many women become the one long before they consciously choose leadership. They become the one who notices what is missing, the one who fills the gap, the one who keeps things from falling apart when circumstances become uncertain.

Early competence is often rewarded with quiet expectation. Reliability becomes an assignment without ever being formally named. Over time, leadership stops being about influence and slowly becomes about constant availability. Not because anyone clearly defined it that way, but because the pattern was never interrupted.

What accumulates in this space is invisible labor. Emotional management. Anticipation. Problem-solving that no one formally asked for, but everyone depends on. The work exists between responsibilities, yet it holds everything together.

Research on women and leadership consistently shows that women are more likely to carry informal, unseen, and uncompensated responsibilities. This does not happen in identical roles or titles, but the pattern is recognizable. When systems falter, women stabilize. When others disengage, women compensate. When something needs to be held together, women are often expected to hold it.

Overcommitment grows from this environment. Not always from ambition, but from fear. Fear that if you do not step in, something important will be left undone. Fear that the family will unravel, the team will struggle, or the work will stall.

Leadership begins to look less like discernment and more like endurance.

Being "The One"

Being "the one" describes the role a person quietly steps into when others begin to rely on them to notice, solve, and stabilize what is missing or unresolved. The one is the person who sees what others overlook, who senses tension before it becomes visible, and who instinctively steps forward to keep things functioning.

This role is rarely formally assigned. It emerges when someone consistently demonstrates reliability and initiative. A person helps once, then again, and gradually others begin to expect that same response.

The one becomes the person people call first when something needs to be solved, organized, or repaired. The one who absorbs confusion and brings clarity. The one who stabilizes environments when they begin to shift.

Being the one can feel empowering because it reflects capability and trust. Yet the role can quietly grow larger than intended. The more dependable a person becomes, the more responsibility is placed on their shoulders.

What began as a moment of leadership can gradually become an expectation of constant availability.

Leadership Labor

Leadership labor refers to the visible and invisible work required to guide people, sustain systems, and maintain stability in complex environments. Some aspects of leadership labor are obvious. They include planning, decision-making, organizing work, and providing direction.

Much of leadership labor, however, happens quietly. It includes emotional awareness, conflict mediation, morale support, and the constant attention required to keep environments functioning smoothly.

Leaders often hold the emotional climate of the spaces they lead. They recognize when tension enters a room. They sense when communication begins to break down. They intervene early to prevent small problems from becoming larger disruptions.

Leadership labor also involves translating vision into action. Leaders must hold long-term goals while managing daily responsibilities. They carry both direction and stability at the same time.

This work requires emotional intelligence, patience, and sustained attention. Leaders often absorb stress so others can continue performing their roles without interruption.

Because much of this work happens quietly, leadership labor often remains invisible even while it holds entire systems together.

Overcommitment

Overcommitment occurs when responsibilities accumulate beyond what a person can sustain without strain. It rarely happens all at once. Instead, it develops gradually through a series of reasonable decisions.

Each commitment may appear manageable on its own—a request for support, a meeting that needs leadership, a responsibility that requires attention. Over time, those commitments multiply.

For people who are capable and dependable, expectations increase quickly. Others notice their effectiveness and begin to rely on it. Opportunities and obligations continue to grow.

Overcommitment can also come from internal expectations. A strong sense of responsibility, care for others, or desire for excellence can make it difficult to decline new responsibilities.

When commitments accumulate without limits, exhaustion begins to appear. Energy becomes divided among too many responsibilities. Reflection and rest become rare.

The work continues, but the weight grows heavier.

Why We Carry It

Many women carry the burden of being the one because responsibility was modeled as strength. From an early age, reliability was praised. The ability to solve problems, care for others, and remain steady in the face of difficulty became a valued trait.

When someone consistently demonstrates competence, people naturally begin to rely on them. Trust grows. Expectations follow. Over time, the person who once volunteered support becomes the person others assume will provide it.

Leadership roles often intensify this pattern. Leaders are expected to respond quickly, make decisions, and provide stability during uncertainty. Because they care about the people and environments they serve, they continue stepping forward even when the responsibility becomes heavy.

Cultural expectations also reinforce this dynamic. Many women are encouraged to be accommodating, responsible, and attentive to others' needs. Helping becomes natural. Carrying extra responsibility becomes familiar.

Eventually, the role becomes internalized. Being dependable becomes part of identity. Letting go of responsibility can feel uncomfortable because reliability has become connected to self-worth.

There is also a quiet belief that if you do not step in, something important may fall apart. That belief keeps the pattern in place.

What This Bag Costs

Carrying the role of the one, combined with leadership labor and overcommitment, creates a quiet form of exhaustion. From the outside, a person may appear capable, composed, and organized. Internally, the constant responsibility slowly drains emotional and physical energy.

The cost often appears gradually. Long periods of attention and decision-making leave little space for rest. Creativity becomes limited because energy is directed toward maintaining stability rather than imagining new possibilities.

Joy can begin to shrink when every moment is filled with responsibility. Even activities that once felt energizing may begin to feel like additional obligations.

Relationships can also feel the strain. When someone is always responsible for keeping things functioning, they may feel isolated within their own competence. Others appreciate their strength but may not recognize the support they themselves need.

Leadership becomes heavier when responsibility is not shared. The leader becomes the center point for every decision, every problem, and every moment of uncertainty. Without collaboration, leadership turns into constant maintenance rather than thoughtful guidance.

Over time, the highest cost becomes invisibility. The strength of the person remains visible, but the weight behind that strength often goes unnoticed.

The result is a quiet imbalance. One person carries stability for many.

Moving Forward

Being the one may have been how leadership first appeared in your life. It may have been the way you discovered your ability to guide, organize, and create stability. Those strengths are real and valuable.

But leadership does not require constant self-sacrifice.

Sustainable leadership expands responsibility rather than concentrating it. It invites others into the work. It allows trust to grow beyond a single person.

Sharing responsibility does not weaken leadership. It strengthens it. When others are given space to contribute, the environment becomes more resilient and collaborative.

Boundaries are part of leadership. They create the space necessary for reflection, clarity, and thoughtful decisions. Without boundaries, even the strongest leader eventually becomes overwhelmed.

Being dependable does not require carrying everything alone. Strength is not defined by how much one person can absorb. It is defined by the ability to build systems where responsibility is shared and supported.

Being the one may have been the beginning of your leadership journey.

But leadership grows when you realize you were never meant to be the only one.

Reflection: Being the One, Leadership Labor, and Overcommitment

Pause

Before responding to the prompts, take a moment to notice what thoughts or emotions surfaced while reading.

Guided Prompts

- When did being needed become part of my identity?
- What responsibilities do I carry that were never officially assigned to me?
- How do I respond when support is offered?
- What does leadership cost me physically and emotionally?
- What would it look like to lead with protection instead of pressure?

Journaling

____

____

____

____

____

____

____

____

____

Your impact does not require self-erasure. Awareness is where you begin defining your role on your own terms.

CHAPTER 3

The Quiet Weight of Unspoken Hurt

The Quiet Weight of Unspoken Hurt

Before going any further, pause and consider what you have learned not to say. Many women carry memories of moments when something painful happened, and the response was silence. The silence was not always chosen freely. Often, it was the result of recognizing that speaking the truth might create conflict, discomfort, or misunderstanding. In those moments, words were withheld so the situation could move forward. Responsibilities remained. Relationships continued. Life carried on.

Yet unprocessed pain does not disappear simply because it was not spoken about. It settles into the background of daily life. Silence becomes functional, and composure becomes a kind of emotional currency. Hurt is postponed so responsibilities can continue uninterrupted. Over time, many women become highly skilled at appearing steady while quietly carrying experiences that were never fully acknowledged.

When emotional pain is ignored, it does not vanish. It often reappears in different forms. It may surface in the body through fatigue, tension, or disrupted sleep. It may appear in relationships through guardedness, hesitation, or emotional distance. What was never expressed continues to influence how a woman feels, responds, and moves through the world.

Many women learn early that minimizing their pain keeps situations manageable. They tell themselves that something was not serious, that it could have been worse, or that speaking about it might create unnecessary complications. This pattern often develops gradually. At first, it may be a practical decision. Over time, however, it becomes a habit that shapes how emotional experiences are processed.

The result is a quiet weight that accumulates slowly. Individual experiences may seem manageable when viewed alone, but together they create a deeper emotional burden.

Memories remain present even when they are rarely discussed. Situations that were never resolved continue to exist in the background of daily life.

There are moments when the body signals that something remains unfinished. A tightening in the chest during certain conversations. Unexpected fatigue when a familiar topic arises. A sense of heaviness that appears without a clear explanation. These reactions often reflect emotional experiences that were never fully processed.

Women frequently continue fulfilling their responsibilities even while carrying this quiet weight. They maintain relationships, support others, and lead effectively in their work. From the outside, everything appears stable. Yet internally, something may remain unsettled.

Many women become skilled at compartmentalizing their experiences. Difficult emotions are placed in mental spaces where they can be temporarily set aside. This ability allows life to continue moving forward even during emotionally complex situations. However, what is compartmentalized rarely disappears completely.

Memories often return unexpectedly. A phrase someone says may echo a painful moment from the past. A familiar situation may trigger a reaction that feels stronger than the present moment alone would justify. Emotional residue from earlier experiences continues to influence perception and response long after the original event has passed.

Sometimes these emotions surface during periods of stillness. When life slows down, the feelings that were postponed may become clearer. Sadness that once seemed manageable may feel heavier. Anger that was dismissed may become easier to recognize. Questions may arise about why certain experiences were never acknowledged.

This process can feel surprising or confusing. Many women believe they have already moved beyond certain experiences, only to discover that unresolved emotions remain connected to them. Moving forward without acknowledgment is not the same as healing.

Healing begins with allowing experiences to be named honestly.

What This Chapter Names

This chapter names the invisible bag of unspoken hurt. Research on trauma, grief, and women's mental health consistently shows that women are more likely to internalize emotional pain to preserve stability and connection. While experiences vary widely, a common pattern emerges in which women absorb hurt quietly so that relationships and environments can remain comfortable.

Unspoken hurt includes grief that was never given space to be expressed, trauma that occurred without language to describe it, disappointment that was never addressed, and relationships that ended without explanation or closure. Many women carry memories of conversations that never happened and apologies that were never offered. They remember moments when something important shifted, yet no one paused long enough to acknowledge the impact.

Sometimes the experiences involved are not dramatic enough to be recognized as trauma. Yet they remain meaningful. Being dismissed, misunderstood, or unsupported during important moments can leave lasting emotional impressions. These experiences accumulate over time.

Silence becomes a strategy that allows life to continue functioning. It prevents conflict and protects relationships. However, what remains unspoken does not become inactive. It continues to influence emotional responses and personal perceptions.

Healing in this context is not about rushing toward resolution. Healing begins with acknowledgment. It involves recognizing what occurred and allowing those experiences to exist honestly rather than minimizing their significance.

How This Bag Shows Up

Unspoken hurt often appears as silence that resembles strength. Women carry painful experiences quietly while continuing to meet responsibilities and expectations. Emotional restraint becomes normal. Language becomes careful and measured.

Many women develop the habit of minimizing their feelings to keep situations stable. Statements such as "I'm fine," "It wasn't that serious," or "It's okay" may be used even when something internally feels unresolved.

This invisible bag often includes unresolved situations. Conversations that never occurred. Relationships that ended without a clear explanation. Interactions where something meaningful was left unaddressed.

Internally, women may replay certain moments repeatedly, wondering what could have been said differently or how the situation might have changed. Externally, they continue to appear composed and capable.

Another way this bag appears is through the emotional weight of other people's pain. Women often absorb the experiences of those around them. They listen to difficult stories, provide comfort, and offer stability without having opportunities to process the emotional impact of what they have heard.

This may include carrying shame that does not belong to them, feeling embarrassed about situations they did not create, or assuming responsibility for conflicts that were not theirs to resolve.

In daily life, unspoken hurt can appear through people-pleasing behaviors, emotional monitoring, and difficulty expressing personal needs. Many women find it challenging to name disappointment, anger, or grief, especially when doing so might disrupt harmony.

Over time, the body may begin to carry what the voice has not expressed. Physical tension, fatigue, headaches, disrupted sleep, and a persistent sense of heaviness can reflect emotional experiences that were never processed openly.

In leadership and professional environments, this bag may show up as emotional distance or guardedness. A woman may continue leading effectively while feeling disconnected from parts of her own experience. Creativity may narrow, and decisions may become more cautious.

Because this pattern develops gradually, the weight of unspoken hurt can become difficult to recognize. Silence begins to feel normal, and endurance begins to feel like maturity.

Why We Carry It

Women often carry this bag because silence once provided safety. Research on trauma and relational dynamics suggests that many women learned early in life that expressing pain could lead to criticism, conflict, dismissal, or rejection. Remaining quiet often felt like the safest option.

Silence protected relationships and preserved belonging. It allowed situations to stabilize without further disruption.

Cultural expectations also reinforce this pattern. Women are frequently praised for patience, composure, and forgiveness. They are encouraged to move forward quickly and maintain harmony even when something painful has occurred.

As a result, emotional endurance often becomes more socially acceptable than emotional honesty.

Another reason women carry unspoken hurt is relational loyalty. Many women hesitate to expose painful experiences because they do not want to harm or embarrass others. They remain silent to preserve family unity, friendships, or professional relationships.

Over time, silence becomes familiar. It begins as a safety strategy and gradually becomes a habit.

What This Bag Costs

Carrying unspoken hurt creates an emotional deficit. When pain is suppressed rather than processed, it continues to consume emotional energy. Maintaining composure requires effort, and that effort slowly drains internal resources.

Women may appear strong and composed while feeling internally exhausted or disconnected from themselves. Emotional distance may increase as a way of protecting against further hurt.

The impact does not remain limited to the individual. When pain has no language, communication within relationships becomes more difficult. Honesty and intimacy can decline, and resentment may quietly replace openness.

In leadership environments, unspoken hurt can reduce clarity and creativity. Decision-making may become cautious rather than bold. Collaboration may feel strained when emotional openness feels unsafe.

Over time, self-abandonment can become normalized. Women may question whether their experiences were significant enough to deserve attention. They may minimize their feelings or convince themselves that remaining silent is the responsible choice.

However, pain that remains unnamed continues to influence behavior and perception.

Release does not have to occur dramatically. This bag can be set down gradually through conversation, counseling, journaling, prayer, or trusted support. It can also begin with a simple acknowledgment of what was previously left unsaid.

Allowing pain to be named removes the power it holds in silence. When experiences are acknowledged honestly, they no longer need to operate quietly in the background.

Healing begins when truth is finally allowed to speak.

Reflection: The Quiet Weight of Unspoken Hurt

Pause

Before responding to the prompts, take a moment to notice what thoughts or emotions surfaced while reading.

Guided Prompts

- What have I learned to survive by not saying?
- Where does my body hold what my voice has not released?
- What pain have I minimized to remain functional?
- What form of healing feels safest right now?
- What would compassion toward my pain look like?

Journaling

What is acknowledged can begin to heal.

CHAPTER 4

When Carrying Becomes Harmful

When Carrying Becomes Harmful

Pushing through pain is not resilience. Listening is.

Your body is not betraying you. It is communicating. Long before language forms, the body tells the truth. You are allowed to slow down long enough to hear the whole story.

Pause for a moment and notice what your body has been trying to say.

Many women never recognize the exact moment when carrying becomes harmful because there is no clear line. No warning. No permission slip. Harm develops gradually and quietly, much like the invisible bags themselves. Fatigue turns into chronic exhaustion. Stress settles into illness. What begins as pushing through eventually collapses.

Women are often praised for ignoring discomfort. Headaches are dismissed. Sleep deprivation is normalized. Irritability is rationalized. Pain becomes background noise. The body is treated as something to override rather than attend to.

Endurance crosses into harm when the body must intervene because the mind has learned not to listen.

What This Chapter Names

This chapter names the invisible bag of chronic overload. Research on burnout, stress-related illness, and women's health consistently shows that women are more likely to experience prolonged stress without adequate recovery. Burnout is not sudden. It is cumulative. It is the result of carrying too much for too long without relief.

Self-neglect rarely begins as neglect. It starts as a postponement. Needs are delayed. Rest is deferred. Signals are ignored because something else feels more urgent. Over time, this pattern becomes normal. Functioning becomes the goal. Flourishing becomes optional.

In this book, capacity is defined as the ability to function without harm. When capacity is exceeded repeatedly, the body intervenes. This intervention is not a failure. It is wisdom.

How This Bag Shows Up

This bag shows up first as subtle exhaustion. Women notice they are tired even after rest, stretched even when nothing new has been added. What once felt manageable now feels heavy. The body begins to whisper before it ever has to shout.

It shows up as pushing through physical and emotional signals that were meant to protect. Headaches are ignored. Sleep disruption is normalized. Irritability is rationalized. Women learn to override discomfort because stopping has never felt like an option. Pain becomes background noise rather than information.

This bag often contains accumulated stress, unresolved trauma, and emotional labor carried for too long without relief. Women may be holding grief they never processed, responsibility that never shifted, or pressure that never eased. Over time, the body becomes the final place where everything lands.

In daily life, this bag shows up as chronic fatigue, brain fog, emotional numbness, or constant tension. Women may feel disconnected from their own bodies, moving through days on autopilot. Joy becomes intermittent. Presence feels difficult to sustain.

It also shows up as illness without a clear cause: migraines, digestive issues, anxiety, depression, autoimmune responses, high blood pressure, or frequent colds. These are not random failures of the body. They are cumulative responses to the carrying capacity.

In relationships, this bag can manifest as withdrawal, impatience, or an emotional shutdown. Women may still show up physically while feeling absent emotionally. Resentment builds quietly. Intimacy feels harder to access because energy has been depleted elsewhere.

In leadership and work, this bag shows up as burnout. Creativity narrows. Decision-making becomes reactive rather than intentional. Women continue to perform while feeling trapped by responsibility. What once felt purposeful now feels unsustainable.

Over time, this bag becomes dangerous as it blends into the background. Functioning replaces flourishing. Survival replaces vitality. The body steps in not as betrayal, but as communication because it can no longer carry what the system has normalized.

Why We Carry It

Women carry this bag because stopping was never modeled as safe. Research on stress, burnout, and women's health consistently shows that women are socialized to prioritize responsibility over recovery. From an early age, many women learned that pushing through was praised, while listening to discomfort was dismissed. Endurance became the standard. Relief became optional.

This bag is reinforced by environments that reward output but ignore cost. Women are often expected to perform without pause, adapt without complaint, and absorb pressure without support. Slowing down can be interpreted as a sign of weakness.

Rest can be misread as laziness. Listening to the body can feel irresponsible when others depend on you.

Many women also carry this bag because they believe everything will collapse if they stop. The family. The job. The team. The relationship. Carrying becomes a way to maintain control in systems that feel fragile or under-resourced. Even when the body signals distress, the fear of letting others down keeps women moving.

This bag is not carried because women are disconnected from their bodies. It is taken because survival taught them to override their needs. Ignoring discomfort once ensured stability. Over time, it became a habit rather than a choice.

What This Bag Costs

Carrying this bag creates a severe emotional impact. Energy is depleted faster than it can be restored. Over time, the cost becomes cumulative and visible—physically, emotionally, relationally, and spiritually. What begins as manageable fatigue evolves into chronic exhaustion, illness, or collapse.

Physically, the cost shows up as persistent fatigue, sleep disruption, headaches, autoimmune responses, high blood pressure, anxiety, depression, and stress-related illness. Emotionally, it appears as numbness, irritability, loss of joy, and a sense of disconnection from oneself. The body becomes the messenger when the voice has learned not to speak.

The cost does not remain contained within the woman. When she is depleted, her capacity to lead, connect, and create is compromised. Leadership becomes reactive rather than intentional. Relationships feel brittle rather than supportive. Presence is replaced by survival mode.

Over time, ignoring the body normalizes self-abandonment. Women begin to distrust their own signals and automatically override their limits. What once felt like strength becomes fragility disguised as resilience.

Release does not require collapse. Listening can begin with one boundary, one rest period, one honest acknowledgment. It can also arrive through a forced stop, burnout, illness, or emotional shutdown. Neither is failure. Both are signals that the body can no longer carry what the system has normalized.

Both gradual release and clean breaks are valid. What matters is recognizing that continuing to override the body causes harm that cannot be sustained indefinitely.

Listening to your body is not a weakness. It is wisdom arriving on time.

Reflection: When Carrying Becomes Harmful

Pause

Before responding to the prompts, take a moment to notice what thoughts or emotions surfaced while reading.

Guided Prompts

- What physical or emotional signals have I learned to ignore?
- How has pushing through been rewarded in my life?
- What feels unsustainable even if it looks successful?
- Where am I functioning but not flourishing?
- What would it mean to trust my body instead of overriding it?

Journaling

___

___

___

___

___

___

___

___

___

Awareness is the first form of protection.

CHAPTER 5

Letting Go as Leadership

Letting Go as Leadership

Releasing what drains you is an act of leadership, not a sign of failure.

Many women were taught that strength means holding on, holding the weight, holding the role, and holding everything together at any cost. Over time, endurance is mistaken for excellence, and exhaustion is taken as proof of commitment.

Before we go any further, pause and notice what you are afraid to release.

For many women, letting go feels more dangerous than carrying on. Carrying has become evidence of competence, loyalty, and leadership. Releasing feels like risking collapse, judgment, or becoming unnecessary. What often goes unnamed is the quiet truth many women already know: leadership that requires self-destruction is not leadership at all.

Release is authority. Authority is the ability to set healthy boundaries, to decide where your energy belongs, and to say no without apology. Letting go is not abandonment. It is discernment. It is choosing alignment over obligation and sustainability over sacrifice.

This chapter reframes leadership not as how much you can carry, but how wisely you choose what remains in your hands. You are allowed to release.

What This Chapter Names

This chapter names the invisible bag of overattachment. Overattachment is not about weakness or lack of boundaries. It is about responsibility held too long, roles outgrown but not released, and relationships sustained by obligation rather than mutuality.

Research on leadership sustainability shows that women are more likely to remain in draining roles because they feel personally responsible for outcomes long after their capacity has been exceeded. Letting go is often framed as abandonment, failure, or selfishness rather than wisdom.

Letting go is defined as a leadership decision that protects clarity, energy, and integrity.

How This Bag Shows Up

This bag shows up as staying longer than is healthy. Women remain in roles, relationships, and responsibilities that no longer fit because leaving feels dangerous. What began as commitment slowly becomes overattachment. Carrying continues not because the role is aligned, but because releasing it feels like risking collapse, judgment, or loss of identity.

It shows up as difficulty letting go, even when the cost is clear. Women feel responsible for outcomes long after their capacity has been exceeded. They continue to manage, fix, and hold together what should have been shared, transitioned, or ended. Delegation feels uncomfortable. Stepping back feels irresponsible. Rest triggers guilt rather than relief.

This bag often contains unwanted burdens inherited through loyalty. Women carry emotional responsibility for people who no longer reciprocate, systems that no longer support them, and missions that have quietly shifted away from mutuality. They stay because they feel irreplaceable, even when that feeling is what drains them.

In daily life, this bag shows up as anxiety when not needed. Stillness feels unsafe. Space feels unfamiliar. Women may find themselves filling their time with tasks, caretaking, or problem-solving to avoid the discomfort of letting go. Carrying becomes a habit rather than a choice.

In relationships, this bag appears as emotional overextension. Women stay connected out of obligation rather than alignment. They carry unresolved guilt, secondhand responsibility, and the emotional weight of keeping relationships intact—even when intimacy has already eroded.

In leadership and work, this bag shows up as burnout disguised as commitment. Women remain in positions that require constant self-sacrifice because leaving feels like failure. Vision is replaced by maintenance. Authority is confused with endurance. What once felt meaningful begins to feel heavy.

Over time, this bag becomes invisible because it is normalized. Carrying too much feels like leadership. Letting go feels like a loss. What is rarely named is that leadership without release eventually costs clarity, creativity, and integrity.

Why We Carry It

Women carry this bag because letting go has been framed as failure rather than discernment. Research on the sustainability of women's leadership shows that women are often evaluated not only on outcomes but also on how much of themselves they give. Over giving becomes an expectation. Endurance becomes evidence of commitment. Stepping back becomes suspect.

This bag is reinforced by systems that reward availability and penalize boundaries. Women learn that releasing responsibility may lead to judgment, loss of trust, or diminished relevance. Letting go feels risky when identity has been built around being indispensable. Carrying becomes a means of maintaining safety in roles where support is inconsistent or conditional.

Many women also carry this bag because responsibility has been confused with loyalty. They stay in roles, relationships, and commitments long after alignment has ended because leaving feels like abandonment. The fear of disappointing others outweighs the cost of staying depleted. Over time, holding on feels easier than facing the discomfort of release.

This bag is not carried because women lack courage. It is taken because they were taught that leadership requires unlimited sacrifice. Letting go challenges narratives that equate worth with endurance and control.

What This Bag Costs

Carrying this bag creates an emotional deficit account. Energy is spent maintaining what no longer aligns, rather than cultivating what could sustain. Women may feel stagnant, resentful, and disconnected from their purpose. Growth is delayed. Movement becomes maintenance.

The cost is self-abandonment. Creativity narrows. Curiosity fades. Leadership shifts from vision to preservation. Relationships remain intact on the surface while intimacy erodes underneath. What once felt meaningful becomes heavy.

The cost does not stay contained within the woman. When responsibility is not released, others are prevented from developing capacity. Dependency replaces development. Teams stall. Relationships become unbalanced. What was meant to help ultimately ends up limiting everyone involved.

Over time, holding on out of fear normalizes depletion. Women begin to equate exhaustion with loyalty and struggle with guilt when they take time for themselves. Alignment is sacrificed to obligation.

Release does not require rapture. Letting go can happen gradually through setting boundaries, delegating, and having honest conversations. It can also arrive through a clean break. Both are valid. What matters is recognizing that leadership built on depletion cannot be sustained.

Reflection: Letting Go as Leadership

Pause

Before responding to the prompts, take a moment to notice what thoughts or emotions surfaced while reading.

Guided Prompts

- What am I holding onto out of fear rather than purpose?
- Where has responsibility replaced alignment?
- What boundary have I delayed too long?
- How would my leadership change with more space?
- What deserves my energy now?

Journaling

____

____

____

____

____

____

____

____

____

Letting go creates alignment and sets boundaries. You don't need permission.

PART III: RELEASING AND REDEFINING

Recognition and reflection prepare the ground for change. Once a woman understands the invisible bags she has been carrying and the weight they hold, a new question emerges: what does it mean to put some of them down?

For many women, releasing weight feels unfamiliar. Responsibilities that once protected relationships or sustained environments may now feel deeply connected to identity. The role of being dependable, strong, or constantly available may have shaped how others see them and how they see themselves.

Because of this, letting go rarely happens suddenly. Release often begins with a small decision. A boundary that is spoken of for the first time. A responsibility that is reconsidered. A moment of honesty about what can no longer be sustained.

These decisions may seem small on the surface, but they represent meaningful shifts. They interrupt patterns that may have existed for years or even decades. They create space where constant obligation once lived.

This section focuses on redefining what it means to live without unnecessary weight. Redefinition does not mean abandoning responsibility or disconnecting from others. Instead, it means recognizing that responsibility can exist without constant self-sacrifice.

When invisible bags are released, space begins to appear. Space for clarity. Space for creativity. Space for rest and reflection. Many women discover that when the weight they carry for others is set down, their own voice becomes easier to hear.

Redefining strength is an important part of this process. Strength is no longer measured by endurance alone. It begins to include discernment, boundaries, and the ability to share responsibility with others.

Letting go also allows relationships to evolve. When one person stops carrying everything, others are invited to develop their own capacity. Teams become more collaborative. Families become more balanced. Leadership becomes more sustainable.

Transformation does not require abandoning connection or responsibility. Instead, it invites balance, intention, and honesty about what is truly yours to carry.

What remains after release is not emptiness. It is clear. It is the freedom to carry only what aligns with your values, your capacity, and your well-being.

Part III explores how women move from endurance to intention. It examines what it means to rebuild confidence, redefine strength, and choose a life in which responsibility is balanced with self-care.

When unnecessary weight is released, something important becomes possible.

A life that is not defined by what you carry, but by how you choose to live.

CHAPTER 6

Rebuilding Confidence, Worth, and Capacity

Rebuilding Confidence, Worth, and Capacity

Worth is not something you earn through exhaustion; it exists first. You are allowed to rebuild. Confidence grows when strain is removed. You are allowed to have enough.

Before we go any further, pause and notice how you have learned to measure your worth.

For many women, confidence has been confused with productivity, availability, and endurance. Being capable became proof of value. Being busy became evidence of importance. Over time, worth became something to earn rather than something to inhabit. This chapter invites a different understanding: rebuilding is not about becoming more. It is about reclaiming what was already there before carrying everything from you.

Rebuilding does not happen all at once. It happens in moments of honesty, rest, and reorientation. It occurs when women stop using depletion as proof of dedication and begin trusting themselves again.

How This Bag Shows Up

This bag shows up as constant self-monitoring. Women measure their worth by how much they accomplish, how available they are, and how useful they remain to others. Rest feels uncomfortable. Stillness feels unearned. Confidence rises and falls based on productivity rather than self-trust.

It shows up as over functioning disguised as ambition. Women take on more than is sustainable, believing that effort proves value. They push past capacity, minimize exhaustion, and delay their own care because slowing down feels like failure. Being busy becomes evidence of importance.

This bag often includes unwanted burdens tied to identity roles, expectations, and responsibilities that were never consciously chosen but quietly accepted. Women may carry secondhand pressure from family, work, or culture to "do more," "be more," or "hold it together," even when the cost is internal erosion.

In daily life, this bag shows up as difficulty resting without guilt, perfectionism, and chronic comparison. Women question themselves when they pause. They doubt their competence when they are not producing. Accomplishments are minimized while mistakes are magnified. Confidence becomes fragile because it depends on external feedback.

In relationships, this bag appears as over giving to maintain a sense of worth. Women show up as helpers, fixers, and supporters while neglecting their own needs. They may fear that if they stop contributing, they will become invisible or less lovable.

In leadership and work, this bag shows up as fear of being replaced, overlooked, or exposed. Women hesitate to delegate, take time off, or set boundaries because productivity has become tied to their sense of security. Leadership becomes performative rather than grounded.

In the body, this bag shows up as chronic fatigue, tension, irritability, and emotional depletion. The nervous system remains activated because worth feels conditional and always at risk. Ease feels unfamiliar. Calm feels undeserved.

Over time, this bag becomes invisible because it is normalized. Exhaustion looks like dedication. Over functioning looks like excellence. What is rarely acknowledged is how confidence slowly erodes when worth is continually proven rather than trusted.

Why We Carry It

Women carry this bag because it's worth was made conditional long before they had the language to challenge it. Research on women, self-esteem, and socialization shows that girls are often praised for being helpful, agreeable, and capable rather than for being whole. Approval becomes currency. Productivity becomes proof of value. Rest becomes something to earn rather than something to expect.

This bag is reinforced by systems that reward output over presence. Women learn that being busy signals importance and that slowing down risk's invisibility. Confidence becomes externalized, tied to performance reviews, praise, usefulness, and the amount accomplished. Over time, effort replaces worth, and exhaustion becomes evidence of commitment.

Many women also carry this bag because exhaustion feels familiar. When depletion has been normalized, ease can feel unsafe. Rest can feel suspicious. Letting go of constant striving may feel like losing identity rather than reclaiming it. Carrying becomes a way to stay anchored in environments that rarely offer unconditional affirmation.

Women are also taught that rebuilding must follow collapse. They believe they must break before they can restore. This belief keeps them carrying longer than is sustainable, postponing healing until something forces them to let go.

This bag is not carried because women doubt their inherent value. It is taken because value was repeatedly linked to what they could provide, rebuilding challenges that association and disruption often come before relief.

What This Bag Costs

Carrying this bag creates a persistent deficit in emotional accounts. Women become productive but disconnected, capable but depleted. They succeed outwardly while feeling uncertain internally. Confidence fluctuates based on external feedback rather than self-trust.

The cost is joy, creativity, and spaciousness. Women lose access to ease, curiosity, and pleasure. Life becomes transactional. Energy is spent proving worth rather than experiencing presence. Leadership becomes driven by fear of inadequacy rather than by clarity and vision.

The cost does not stay contained within the woman. When conditional worth drives behavior, over functioning becomes normalized. Teams and families absorb the strain. Capacity shrinks across systems as sustainability is sacrificed for output. What looks like dedication slowly becomes quiet depletion for everyone involved.

Over time, women begin to distrust themselves even as they succeed. Rest feels undeserved. Stillness feels unproductive. Self-trust erodes as performance replaces intuition. What once felt like ambition becomes constant pressure.

Rebuilding does not require collapse. Capacity can be restored gradually through rest, support, boundaries, and self-compassion or through a decisive shift in how worth is defined. Both are valid. What matters is choosing restoration over repetition.

You do not have to earn your place by exhausting yourself. You are allowed to rebuild at your own pace.

Reflection: Rebuilding Confidence, Worth, and Capacity

Pause

Before responding to the prompts, take a moment to notice what thoughts or emotions surfaced while reading.

Guided Prompts

- How do I currently measure my worth?
- When do I feel most valuable, and why?
- Where has productivity replaced presence?
- What support could expand my capacity?
- What version of myself emerges when I stop performing my worth?

Journaling

Carrying less makes room for growth.

CHAPTER 7

Choosing Yourself Without Guilt

Choosing Yourself Without Guilt

Choosing yourself is not betrayal; it is repair. You are allowed to choose yourself. Choosing yourself restores what is erased. You are permitted to live lighter.

Before we go any further, pause and notice what choosing yourself brings up.

For many women, choosing themselves feels dangerous. Guilt rises immediately, not because the choice is wrong, but because it disrupts a lifetime of conditioning. Women who have built their identities around holding everything together often experience self-prioritization as abandonment. The discomfort is real, but it is not evidence of harm. It is evidence of change.

Choosing yourself is not a moment. It is a practice. It is the ongoing decision to stop disappearing in the service of everyone else's comfort. It is the willingness to believe that the world does not need you exhausted to survive.

What This Chapter Names

This chapter names the invisible bag of guilt. Research on women, caregiving, leadership, and self-prioritization shows that women are far more likely than men to associate self-care with harm to others. Guilt becomes the mechanism that keeps women carrying on long after the cost is clear.

This bag is reinforced by messages that suggest good women are selfless, available, and endlessly giving. Choosing yourself is framed as selfish rather than as sustainable. In this book, guilt is defined as emotional discomfort that arises when long-standing patterns are disrupted, not as a signal that harm is being done.

Choosing yourself is reframed here as a responsibility for your own well-being, not as a rejection of others.

How This Bag Shows Up

This bag shows up as hesitation the moment a woman considers choosing herself. Relief appears first, then guilt follows immediately. Women feel the pull to rest, to step back, to say no, or to change direction, and just as quickly, they question themselves. Am I being selfish? Am I abandoning someone? Am I wrong for wanting this? The internal debate becomes automatic.

This bag often includes emotional baggage from relationships that did not work but were never fully released. Women remain emotionally tethered long after circumstances have changed, continuing to explain, accommodate, or carry responsibility for how others feel. They carry guilt for endings, boundaries, and decisions that were necessary but uncomfortable.

It also shows up as carrying secondhand guilt. Women absorb disappointment that does not belong to them. They manage other people's reactions, emotions, and expectations in advance, adjusting their choices to minimize others' discomfort, even when it costs them peace.

In daily life, this bag shows up as saying yes while feeling resentment, postponing needs indefinitely, and framing self-care as temporary rather than essential. Women may minimize their own exhaustion, telling themselves that others have it worse or that now is not the right time to look after themselves.

In relationships, this bag appears as over giving driven by fear of disapproval or abandonment. Women remain available out of habit rather than alignment. They struggle to leave situations that drain them because guilt convinces them that staying is kinder than telling the truth.

In leadership and work, this bag shows up as difficulty redefining roles, stepping back, or prioritizing well-being. Women fear being perceived as less committed if they choose sustainability over sacrifice. Leadership decisions become filtered through guilt rather than clarity.

In the body, this bag shows up as tension, anxiety, shallow breathing, and emotional fatigue. Even moments of rest feel uneasy. Peace feels suspicious. Choosing yourself can feel heavier than carrying the burden itself.

Over time, this bag becomes invisible because guilt has been normalized. Discomfort is mistaken for wrongdoing. Self-abandonment feels responsible. What is rarely named is that guilt is not evidence of harm; it is evidence that old conditioning is being interrupted.

Why We Carry It

Women carry this bag because guilt has been taught as a moral compass rather than an emotional response. Research on women, caregiving, leadership, and social conditioning shows that women are far more likely to associate self-prioritization with harm to others. From an early age, many women learned that goodness was measured by sacrifice and availability. Choosing yourself disrupts that training.

This bag is reinforced by narratives that frame selflessness as virtue and boundaries as betrayal. Women are often taught to seek peace without apology, to move on without closure, and to absorb hurt rather than question it. They learn not to ask why someone caused harm, but to manage the discomfort quietly and continue showing up. Guilt becomes the mechanism that keeps women carrying on long after alignment has ended.

Many women also carry this bag because their identities were built around being reliable, nurturing, and needed. Choosing yourself threatens those roles. It raises fears of being misunderstood, judged, or abandoned. Even when a choice brings relief, guilt rushes in as a familiar warning: This is wrong. This is selfish. This will cost you love.

This bag is not carried because women lack self-trust. It is taken because guilt was conditioned as a form of protection. Discomfort became the signal to return to self-abandonment rather than move toward freedom.

What This Bag Costs

Carrying this bag creates a persistent deficit in the emotional account. Women live in a state of internal conflict, torn between what they need and what they believe others expect. Over time, this tension becomes exhaustion, resentment, and emotional withdrawal.

The cost is authenticity. Women lose access to their desires, boundaries, and voice. Decisions are filtered through fear of disappointment rather than clarity. Relationships remain intact on the surface, while intimacy erodes beneath the surface because honesty has been delayed too long.

The cost does not stay contained within the woman. When guilt drives behavior, self-abandonment is normalized. Others learn to rely rather than grow. What feels like kindness slowly becomes quiet harm. Leadership becomes constrained by fear of disapproval rather than guided by vision.

Over time, women begin to distrust their own needs. Relief is questioned. Peace feels suspicious. Choosing yourself becomes something to justify rather than inhabit. Carrying guilt becomes heavier than carrying the burden itself.

Release does not require explanation. This bag can be put down gradually through small acts of self-honoring or through decisive change. Both are valid. What matters is that guilt no longer gets the final say.

Choosing yourself is not abandonment. It is a repair. Choosing yourself does not take anything away. It gives something back. You are allowed to choose yourself without apology.

Reflection: Choosing Yourself Without Guilt

Pause

Before responding to the prompts, take a moment to notice what thoughts or emotions surfaced while reading.

Guided Prompts

- What emotions surface when I imagine putting myself first?
- Where did I learn that self-sacrifice equals love?
- How has guilt influenced my decisions?
- What would change if guilt became information, not instruction?
- Who am I becoming as I let go of the need to save everything?

Journaling

____

____

____

____

____

____

____

____

____

You are allowed to choose yourself.

CHAPTER 8

You Were Never Meant to Carry It All

You Were Never Meant to Carry It All

Carrying everything is often mistaken for strength. Many women learn early that being dependable means stepping forward when something is missing. They solve problems quickly, stabilize environments, and protect the people around them from instability. Over time, these actions become habits. What begins as care gradually becomes expectation.

Responsibility expands quietly. A woman who consistently demonstrates competence becomes the first-person others rely on. She remembers what others forget. She anticipates what others overlook. She resolves what others avoid. The system begins to function around her reliability.

As this pattern develops, the belief begins to form that everything depends on her. If she stops carrying so much, something important may fall apart. This belief can feel convincing because her efforts have often been the reason situations have remained stable.

Yet the ability to hold everything together is not proof that one person should carry everything. It is simply evidence that she has been willing to step forward when others hesitated.

Many women have been conditioned to believe that strength means absorbing pressure without complaint. They are praised for endurance. They are admired for how much they can manage. They are respected for how calmly they carry heavy responsibilities.

But endurance has limits.

Even the strongest leaders were never meant to sustain constant pressure alone. Families, organizations, and communities function best when responsibility is shared among many hands rather than resting on one pair of shoulders.

When one person carries everything, the system adapts around that pattern. Others begin to rely on her effort rather than building their own capacity. Over time, what looks like competence becomes imbalanced. Responsibility becomes concentrated rather than shared.

The woman carrying everything often develops a constant sense of vigilance. She monitors situations, anticipates problems, and prepares solutions before anyone else notices the issue. While this skill can be valuable, it can also create a life where rest feels unsafe and responsibility never truly ends.

Over responsibility often develops through overcompensation. A woman may step in to prevent disappointment, conflict, or failure. She may carry more to ensure a good outcome. She may also do it because she believes no one else will.

Over time, overcompensation becomes invisible. What began as temporary support became permanent responsibility. Others adapt to the pattern. Instead of stepping forward, they rely on the woman who always has.

Leadership slowly becomes maintenance. Instead of guiding others, the leader becomes responsible for stabilizing everything around her. She holds systems together rather than helping them grow.

This chapter invites a different perspective.

Carrying everything may have been necessary during certain seasons of life. It may have protected relationships, stabilized environments, or ensured that important work continued. But necessity should not become permanence.

Responsibility was never meant to erase the person carrying it.

You were never meant to carry it all.

What This Chapter Names

This chapter names the invisible bag of over-responsibility. Research on women, leadership, and caregiving consistently shows that women are more likely to absorb responsibilities beyond their formal roles.

Over-responsibility occurs when one person becomes the stabilizing force for an entire system. The bag forms when competence is repeatedly rewarded with more responsibility. What begins as initiative becomes expectation. What begins as leadership becomes constant pressure.

This bag often includes emotional labor, decision-making, conflict mediation, and logistical management that should be shared among many people.

How This Bag Shows Up

This bag represents constant vigilance. Women who carry it often feel responsible for anticipating problems before they appear. They monitor situations closely and step in quickly to prevent disruption.

In leadership, this bag appears as over functioning. Leaders may feel responsible for outcomes, relationships, morale, and performance simultaneously. Instead of guiding others, they absorb the pressure themselves.

In daily life, this bag appears as chronic overcommitment. Women manage schedules, relationships, emotional needs, and responsibilities across multiple environments. They often feel responsible for maintaining stability in families, friendships, and workplaces.

Why We Carry It

Women carry this bag because responsibility has been framed as strength. Many learned early that being dependable brought approval, trust, and a sense of belonging.

Cultural expectations also reinforce the belief that women should maintain harmony and stability. Stepping forward becomes automatic. Over time, many women fear that if they stop carrying everything, the system will fail or someone will be disappointed.

Carrying more begins to feel safer than letting something fall.

What This Bag Costs

Carrying everything creates exhaustion over time. Energy becomes divided across too many responsibilities. Reflection and rest become rare.

The cost extends beyond the individual. When one person carries everything, others stop developing their own capacity. Teams lose collaboration. Families lose balance. Systems become dependent on one person's endurance.

What appears to be strength slowly becomes fragility.

Releasing unnecessary weight allows systems to grow. Responsibility becomes shared. Leadership becomes sustainable. And the woman who once carried everything begins to reclaim the space she was never meant to lose.

Reflections: You Were Never Meant to Carry It All

Pause

Before responding to the prompts, take a moment to notice what thoughts or emotions surfaced while reading.

Guided Prompts

Where in my life have I been carrying more than my share of responsibility?
What situations lead me to overcompensate for others?
What fears arise when I imagine carrying less?
Where could responsibility be shared more effectively?
How might my leadership change if I trusted others to hold their part?

Journaling

____

____

____

____

____

____

____

____

____

Strength is not proven by how much one person carries. It is revealed by how responsibility is shared.

CHAPTER 9

Carrying It Forward

Carrying It Forward

Releasing invisible weight does not mean life becomes free of responsibility. Responsibility will always exist in leadership, relationships, and community life. What changes is the way responsibility is carried.

Throughout this book, you have explored the invisible bags that often shape women's lives. Some were inherited through generations that equated strength with endurance. Others developed through leadership roles where competence invited increasing expectations.

Over time, these expectations formed patterns. Responsibilities were accepted without question. Emotional labor went unacknowledged. Expectations expanded simply because they had existed for so long.

Recognition is the beginning of change.

When a woman begins to recognize the weight, she has been carrying, she starts to see responsibility differently. Instead of automatically absorbing pressure, she pauses. Instead of stepping forward immediately, she considers whether the responsibility truly belongs to her.

This pause is important.

For women who have spent years being the dependable one, the habit of stepping in quickly can feel automatic. In moments of stress, the instinct to fix, organize, or stabilize may return immediately.

That instinct does not disappear overnight.

Growth requires practice.

Each time a woman chooses to carry only what belongs to her, she strengthens a new pattern. Each time she allows others to step forward, she creates space for shared responsibility.

Over time, leadership begins to change.

Instead of absorbing pressure alone, the leader begins guiding others toward participation. Instead of maintaining stability single-handedly, she builds environments where stability is shared.

Carrying life forward means remembering what you have learned about yourself.

It means protecting the awareness that came through reflection. It means recognizing that responsibility need not disappear for life to become lighter. It only needs to be carried with intention.

The work does not end when the book ends.

It continues in everyday decisions. It appears in the boundaries you maintain, the responsibilities you accept, and the ones you decline.

Over time, these choices reshape the environments you move through. Relationships become more balanced. Leadership becomes more collaborative. Responsibility becomes shared rather than silently absorbed.

Carrying it forward means living with the clarity that you are allowed to carry less and still lead well.

Strength was never meant to be measured by how much one person can hold.

It is measured by how wisely responsibility is shared.

What This Chapter Names

This chapter names the invisible bag of continuation.

Even after women recognize the weight they have been carrying, many return to familiar patterns simply because those habits have been practiced for years.

Continuation is the tendency to revert to old roles of over responsibility, emotional labor, and overcommitment under increased pressure.

Awareness alone does not change patterns. Change requires practicing new responses until they become natural.

How This Bag Shows Up

This bag shows up as returning to familiar roles during moments of stress. Women may find themselves stepping back into over functioning because it feels faster or safer than waiting for others to respond.

In leadership, this bag appears when leaders begin to solve every problem themselves, rather than allowing teams to develop their own capacity.

In daily life, it appears as saying yes automatically, managing others' emotional dynamics, and absorbing responsibilities that could be shared.

Without awareness, the pattern quietly returns.

Why We Carry It

Women carry this bag because familiarity feels safe.

Patterns developed over the years do not disappear quickly. When a woman has spent a long time stabilizing her environment, others may continue expecting her to play that role.

The pressure to return to old habits can be strong.

There is also comfort in what is familiar. Even when the pattern is exhausting, it is known.

Learning to carry life forward requires patience. Each new boundary and each intentional decision help create a different pattern.

What This Bag Costs

Returning to old habits slows the work of transformation.

Women may find themselves repeating cycles of exhaustion, overcommitment, and emotional labor simply because those patterns are familiar.

The cost is not failure. The cost is a delay.

True change happens when new choices are practiced consistently. Each time a woman chooses alignment over overcompensation, she strengthens a healthier pattern.

Over time, responsibility becomes balanced rather than overwhelming.

Leadership becomes sustainable.

And life begins to feel lighter.

Reflections: Carrying It Forward

Before responding to the prompts, notice what thoughts or emotions surfaced as you reached the end of this book.

Guided Prompts

What invisible bags have I begun to release?
What habits will help me remain aware of what I carry?
How has my understanding of leadership and responsibility changed?
Where do I need stronger boundaries moving forward?
What kind of life do I want to build with the space that releasing weight creates?

Journaling

____

____

____

____

____

____

____

____

____

____

You move forward not by carrying everything, but by choosing what truly belongs to you.

Letter to the Reader

Dear Reader,

If you have reached this point, you have traveled through reflections that many women rarely pause long enough to name. You have walked through the quiet terrain of invisible labor, emotional responsibility, endurance, and expectations that often remain hidden beneath the surface of daily life.

Along the way, you may have recognized some of the invisible bags you have carried.

Perhaps you saw yourself as expected to remain strong even when rest was needed. You may have recognized the role of being the one who notices, fixes, stabilizes, and leads without always receiving the support you deserve. Perhaps you recognized moments of unspoken hurt that were never given language yet continued to shape how you move through relationships and responsibilities.

You may also have recognized how these patterns developed.

Inherited strength taught many women to endure without pause. Leadership roles expanded into invisible labor, quietly filling every gap. Silence protected relationships even when it left personal pain unresolved. Over time, endurance began to replace discernment, and carrying everything felt like the only way forward.

This book invited you to pause and examine that pattern.

Part I asked you to recognize the invisible bags that often go unnamed. It explored how inherited expectations, leadership labor, and unspoken hurt become woven into daily life.

Part II invited you to confront the weight those patterns create. It examined how responsibilities that once felt temporary can quietly become permanent. It asked deeper questions about boundaries, identity, and the difference between caring for others and carrying everything for them.

Part III explored the possibility of something different. It considers what it means to release unnecessary weight and redefine strength in ways that include rest, clarity, and shared responsibility.

None of this work happens instantly.

Releasing invisible weight rarely occurs in a single dramatic moment. More often, it begins quietly. It begins with awareness. By noticing what once felt automatic. With questioning responsibilities that were accepted long ago.

Sometimes the first step is simply recognizing that you are allowed to carry less.

If certain pages felt like mirrors, may they continue to bring clarity.

If certain pages feel like permission, may they remind you that boundaries are not weakness.

If certain pages felt like release, may they create space for something new.

You do not have to drop every bag at once. Some may remain for a while longer. Others may become lighter simply because they have been named.

What matters is that you now have language for what you have been carrying.

Strength does not disappear when weight is set down. It becomes more intentional. It becomes the ability to choose what you carry rather than accepting everything that falls into your hands.

As you leave these pages, carry forward what strengthens you.

Leave behind what no longer belongs to you.

And remember this: you were never meant to carry it all alone.

With care,

Dr. Tarcia Gilliam-Parrish

If This Book Met You at a Tender Place

If these pages met you at a tender place, and something here stirred recognition, fatigue, or quiet truth you had not named before, you are not alone.

Invisible bags are often carried without acknowledgement. Many people learn early to hold responsibility, expectation, and emotional weight without questioning whether the load was ever meant for them. Over time, the carrying becomes familiar. It can feel normal to absorb pressure, solve problems, and make space for others while leaving little room for yourself.

When those patterns begin to surface, reflection can bring both relief and discomfort. Realizing how much you have carried may reveal emotions that were set aside to keep moving forward. That awareness is not failure. It is the beginning of clarity.

Some readers may recognize themselves in the weight of inherited expectations. The quiet belief that strength meant continuing to carry without complaint. Others may recognize the habit of holding emotional responsibility for situations that were never theirs to manage.

If these pages helped you see the invisible bags you have been carrying, allow yourself patience as you navigate what that realization brings. Awareness does not require immediate change. Understanding unfolds over time.

Support can appear in many ways. It may come through honest conversations with someone you trust. It may come through writing, reflection, or quiet moments where you allow yourself to notice what you have been holding.

There is no required pace for releasing what was never meant to stay with you.

You are allowed to set down what has become too heavy.

You are allowed to carry less.

You are allowed to choose balance over endurance.

Laying the Bags Down

For many people, strength once meant carrying everything.

It meant holding families together, managing expectations, resolving conflict, and absorbing emotional strain so that others would not have to. Over time, that pattern can become so familiar that it feels like identity.

But strength evolves.

Strength does not require endless carrying. It does not require absorbing every responsibility or solving every problem that appears.

True strength recognizes limits. It understands that not every burden belongs in your hands.

Laying down invisible bags does not erase compassion or responsibility. Instead, it restores balance. It allows you to remain thoughtful, caring, and engaged without carrying weight that was never yours.

Some bags belonged to expectations placed on you long ago.
Some belonged to roles you stepped into without realizing the cost.
Some belonged to situations that required survival but no longer required constant endurance.

Setting those bags down is not abandonment. It is alignment.

Strength, when understood differently, becomes the ability to recognize what is yours to carry and what is not.

It becomes the ability to move through life with steadiness rather than exhaustion.

You do not have to carry everything to prove your strength.

Acknowledgments

This book was shaped by the experiences and reflections of many individuals who have carried responsibility, expectation, and emotional labor in ways that were rarely acknowledged.

I am grateful to the mentors, colleagues, and community members whose insight and honesty continue to deepen conversations about resilience, leadership, and the unseen work that so many people perform every day.

I am also thankful for the students, families, and communities whose perseverance reminds us of that strength often appears in quiet commitment rather than visible recognition.

I extend gratitude to my family, whose love and shared vision continue to inspire the work we do together through Sister Soul Seasonings, our family-owned seasoning company. Their dedication to building something meaningful together reflects the same values of perseverance, connection, and community that shape these pages.

Finally, I thank every reader who approaches this book with an open mind. Your willingness to recognize and reflect on the invisible work you carry helps bring these conversations into the light.

About the Author

Dr. Tarcia Gilliam-Parrish is an educator, author, mentor, and community leader whose work centers on leadership, personal growth, and the often-unseen responsibilities people carry in their personal and professional lives.

She is the co-founder of The Power of Engagement, an organization dedicated to mentorship, leadership development, and community engagement. Through this work, she partners with schools, organizations, and community leaders to support initiatives that strengthen opportunity and connection.

Dr. Gilliam-Parrish also serves as the Director of The Exquisite Pearls of Excellence, a mentoring initiative that supports the growth, confidence, and leadership development of young women.

In addition to her work in education and mentorship, she is part of Sister Soul Seasonings. This family-owned seasoning company celebrates culture, tradition, and the power of building something meaningful together.

Through her writing and leadership, Dr. Gilliam-Parrish continues to encourage thoughtful reflection on resilience, identity, and the invisible work that shapes who we become.

Dr. Tarcia Gilliam-Parrish

Also, by Dr. Tarcia Gilliam-Parrish

Dr. Tarcia Gilliam-Parrish is an educator, author, and leadership voice whose work centers on resilience, identity, leadership, and the unseen emotional labor many women carry. Through reflection and clear insight, her writing invites readers to pause, examine the weight they have been holding, and move forward with clarity, intention, and renewed strength.

The Invisible Work Series

Woman, Interrupted

An exploration of the moments when life unexpectedly shifts direction. This book examines identity after disruption and invites readers to reflect on how interruptions reshape purpose, priorities, and personal understanding.

Invisible Bags

A reflective guide that names the unseen emotional, relational, and leadership burdens many women carry. Through insight and guided reflection, readers are encouraged to recognize the weight they have been carrying and begin releasing what no longer belongs to them.

Invisible Work

The final volume of the series explores the authority that emerges when women reclaim their time, voice, and direction. It focuses on living with intention and leading without unnecessary weight.

The Paper Doll Collection

The Art of Resilience

A visual and reflective work exploring the strength women develop through adversity. Through symbolic imagery and thoughtful commentary, this book examines how resilience forms through experience and how women continue to rebuild, adapt, and grow even after difficult seasons.

The Art of Being Seen

A companion work that explores identity, visibility, and voice. This collection reflects on what it means for women to move beyond expectations and fully inhabit their presence, perspective, and power.

Children's Literature

The Marina James Chronicles

A children's book series that follows the imaginative adventures of Marina James as she learns lessons about curiosity, courage, leadership, and community.

Additional Work

Dr. Gilliam-Parrish's writing often bridges personal reflection and leadership development. Her work is used by educators, mentors, and community leaders who seek thoughtful conversations about responsibility, resilience, and sustainable leadership.

For speaking engagements, educational resources, and updates on upcoming projects, follow Dr. Tarcia Gilliam-Parrish on all social media platforms.

www.ingramcontent.com/pod-product-compliance
Lightning Source LLC
LaVergne TN
LVHW061204120826
845149LV00011B/1899
9781964663210